Customer Care 2.0: Leveraging AI for Exceptional Service

Delroy Briscoe

1

Customer Care 2.0: Leveraging AI for

Exceptional Service

Delroy Briscoe

Chapter 1: Introduction to Customer Care 2.0

The Evolution of Customer Service

The evolution of customer service has been a remarkable journey, re ecting changes in technology, consumer behavior, and business practices. Historically, customer service was largely reactive, with companies responding to inquiries and complaints as they arose. The primary channels of communication were face-to-face interactions, telephone calls, and written correspondence. In this environment, customer service representatives often operated with limited information and resources, leading to inconsistent experiences for consumers. The focus was primarily on resolving issues rather than fostering relationships or anticipating needs.

The advent of the internet in the late 20th century marked a signi cant shift in customer service dynamics. Businesses began to embrace digital communication channels, allowing for faster and more ef cient interactions. Email support emerged as a popular method, enabling companies to handle a higher volume of inquiries without the constraints of traditional phone support. This transition also introduced the concept of self-service, with FAQs and online knowledge bases providing customers with the ability to nd answers independently. As businesses adapted to this new landscape, the importance of timely responses and a customer-centric approach became increasingly evident.

The rise of social media in the 21st century further transformed customer service, creating a public forum for interactions between consumers and brands. Customers began to expect immediate responses to their inquiries and complaints, leading companies to adopt more proactive strategies. Social media platforms became both a channel for customer service and a space for brand reputation management. Businesses that effectively engaged with customers on these platforms were able to build stronger relationships and foster loyalty. As a result, customer service evolved from a purely transactional interaction to a more holistic experience that incorporated brand values and customer engagement.

In recent years, the introduction of arti cial intelligence has ushered in a new era for customer service. AI technologies, such as chatbots and virtual assistants, have enabled companies to provide 24/7 support and address customer inquiries in real time. This shift has not only improved response times but also allowed human representatives to focus on more complex issues that require empathy and critical thinking. AI-driven analytics provide businesses with valuable insights into customer behavior and preferences, enabling them to tailor their services and anticipate needs more effectively. The integration of AI in customer service represents a signi cant advancement in the quest for exceptional service.

Looking ahead, the future of customer service will likely be characterized by a seamless integration of human and AI capabilities. Companies will continue to leverage technology to enhance customer experiences while maintaining the essential human touch that fosters genuine connections. As consumers become more discerning and expect personalized service, businesses will need to adapt by adopting advanced AI tools that can learn and evolve in response to customer interactions. The ongoing evolution of customer service not only highlights the importance of embracing innovation but also emphasizes the need for a strategic approach that prioritizes customer satisfaction and loyalty in an increasingly competitive landscape.

Understanding Customer Expectations

Understanding customer expectations is a crucial aspect of delivering exceptional service, particularly in the context of advanced technologies like arti cial intelligence. As businesses increasingly integrate AI into their customer service operations, it is essential to grasp what customers anticipate from these interactions. Customers today are not only looking for ef ciency but also for personalization, consistency, and a seamless experience across various channels. This understanding forms the foundation for developing AI solutions that genuinely cater to customer needs and enhance satisfaction.

One of the primary expectations customers have is responsiveness. In the digital age, consumers expect immediate answers to their queries, whether through chatbots, virtual assistants, or other AI-driven platforms. Delays in response times can lead to frustration and a negative perception of the brand. Therefore, businesses must ensure that their AI systems are designed to provide timely and accurate responses, thereby fostering a sense of reliability and trust. Furthermore, the integration of AI with human agents can enhance this responsiveness by allowing for quicker resolutions of complex issues.

Personalization is another critical expectation among customers. With the vast amounts of data available, AI can tailor interactions based on individual preferences and past behaviors. Customers appreciate when businesses recognize their unique needs and customize their offerings accordingly. This level of personalization can manifest in various ways, such as recommending products based on previous purchases or addressing customers by name during interactions. By leveraging AI to deliver personalized experiences, companies can signi cantly enhance customer loyalty and satisfaction.

Consistency across all customer touchpoints is also vital. Customers today interact with brands through multiple channels, including social media, websites, and mobile apps. They expect a uniform experience regardless of the platform they choose. AI can help ensure this consistency by providing a centralized database of customer interactions and preferences, enabling seamless transitions between different channels. When customers receive coherent and consistent service, they are more likely to develop a positive relationship with the brand, leading to increased retention and advocacy.

Finally, transparency is an essential component of customer expectations in the realm of AI. As customers engage with AI-driven systems, they want to understand how their data is being used and the rationale behind certain automated decisions. Clear communication regarding data privacy and the limitations of AI solutions can help build trust between customers and businesses. By being transparent about AI processes and outcomes, companies can alleviate concerns and foster a more positive perception of their customer service efforts. This level of openness is crucial for cultivating long-term relationships in an environment where customers are increasingly aware of and concerned about their digital interactions.

The Role of Technology in Customer Care

Technology has fundamentally transformed the landscape of customer care, enabling businesses to provide more ef cient, personalized, and responsive services. At the heart of this transformation is arti cial intelligence (AI), which has emerged as a powerful tool for enhancing customer interactions. AI technologies, such as chatbots, virtual assistants, and predictive analytics, allow companies to streamline their operations and respond to customer inquiries in real-time, paving the way for a more satisfying consumer experience.

One of the most signi cant advancements in customer care is the use of chatbots and virtual assistants. These AI-driven solutions can handle a multitude of customer queries simultaneously, reducing wait times and freeing human agents to tackle more complex issues. By leveraging natural language processing, chatbots can understand and respond to customer requests with remarkable accuracy, providing immediate assistance at any hour of the day. This not only improves customer satisfaction but also helps businesses manage their resources more effectively.

Predictive analytics is another technological advancement that has reshaped customer care. By analyzing customer data and behavior patterns, businesses can anticipate customer needs and tailor their services accordingly. This proactive approach not only enhances the customer experience but also fosters loyalty, as consumers feel valued when their preferences are recognized and catered to. Companies can use insights gained from predictive analytics to re ne their marketing strategies and create personalized offers, further engaging their customer base.

AI technology also plays a crucial role in enhancing the training and performance of customer service agents. By utilizing machine learning algorithms, businesses can analyze interactions between agents and customers, identifying areas for improvement and providing targeted feedback. This data-driven approach to training ensures that agents are well-equipped to handle various customer scenarios, leading to more effective resolutions and a higher level of service. Additionally, AI can assist in monitoring agent performance in real-time, allowing for immediate adjustments and support when necessary.

Furthermore, the integration of AI in customer care fosters a more collaborative environment between technology and human agents. Instead of replacing human interaction, AI serves as a complement, providing agents with the tools and insights they need to excel. This hybrid model not only enhances the overall service quality but also encourages a culture of continuous improvement within organizations. As businesses continue to leverage technology in customer care, the focus remains on creating meaningful interactions that build trust and long-term relationships with customers.

Chapter 2: The Basics of AI in Customer Service

What is Artificial Intelligence?

Arti cial Intelligence (AI) refers to the simulation of human intelligence processes by machines, particularly computer systems. These processes include learning, reasoning, problem-solving, perception, and language understanding. In the context of customer service, AI can signi cantly enhance the ef ciency and effectiveness of service delivery, transforming how businesses interact with their customers. By utilizing advanced algorithms and vast amounts of data, AI systems can analyze customer behavior, predict needs, and provide personalized experiences in real-time.

One of the primary components of AI is machine learning, where systems are trained to recognize patterns in data and improve over time without explicit programming. This capability allows AI to analyze customer interactions, identify trends, and optimize responses based on historical data. For instance, chatbots equipped with machine learning can learn from past conversations to provide more accurate answers to customer queries. This not only streamlines the customer service process but also frees human agents to focus on more complex issues that require emotional intelligence and critical thinking.

Natural language processing (NLP) is another crucial aspect of AI, enabling machines to understand and interpret human language in a way that is both meaningful and contextually relevant. In customer service, NLP facilitates interactions between customers and AI systems, allowing for seamless communication. Through NLP, AI can comprehend customer inquiries and respond appropriately, whether through text or voice. This enhances user experience by providing quick and accurate responses, thereby increasing customer satisfaction and loyalty.

AI also plays a vital role in data analytics, allowing businesses to gather insights from customer interactions and feedback. By analyzing this data, companies can identify pain points in their service delivery and make informed decisions about improvements. Predictive analytics, a subset of AI, can forecast customer behavior based on past interactions, enabling businesses to proactively address customer needs before they arise. This level of foresight is invaluable in creating a customer-centric approach that anticipates and meets expectations.

Ultimately, the integration of AI in customer service not only improves operational ef ciency but also enriches the overall customer experience. As organizations continue to adopt AI technologies, they can provide faster responses, personalized service, and data-driven insights that empower both customers and employees. Embracing AI in customer service is not merely a trend; it represents a fundamental shift towards a more responsive and intelligent service model that can adapt to the evolving needs of customers in a digital age.

Types of AI Technologies Used in Customer Service

Arti cial Intelligence (AI) technologies have transformed customer service by enhancing ef ciency, improving response times, and personalizing customer interactions. One of the most prevalent forms of AI in customer service is chatbots. These automated systems can handle a wide array of customer inquiries, providing instant responses to frequently asked questions. Chatbots can be programmed to operate through various platforms, including websites, messaging apps, and social media. Their ability to learn from previous interactions enables them to deliver increasingly accurate answers over time, thereby reducing the need for human intervention and allowing human agents to focus on more complex issues.

Another signi cant type of AI technology in customer service is Natural Language Processing (NLP). NLP allows machines to understand, interpret, and respond to human language in a way that is both meaningful and contextually relevant. This capability is crucial in customer service, as it enables systems to analyze customer inquiries and provide appropriate responses. NLP algorithms can also be employed to gauge customer sentiment, allowing businesses to tailor their responses based on the emotional tone of the communication. By effectively utilizing NLP, companies can enhance customer satisfaction and foster deeper connections with their clientele.

Voice recognition technology is also becoming increasingly important in customer service. This technology allows customers to interact with service systems through voice commands, facilitating a more natural and intuitive user experience. Voice-activated AI assistants can assist customers with various tasks, such as placing orders, checking account balances, or troubleshooting issues. The growing popularity of smart speakers and mobile devices with voice capabilities has driven the adoption of this technology, making it an essential tool for businesses looking to offer seamless and user-friendly customer interactions.

Predictive analytics represents another powerful AI technology used in customer service. By analyzing historical data and identifying patterns, predictive analytics can help businesses anticipate customer needs and preferences. This proactive approach allows companies to deliver personalized recommendations and solutions before customers even realize they need them. For example, a retail company might use predictive analytics to suggest products to customers based on their previous purchases, enhancing the overall shopping experience and increasing customer loyalty.

Finally, machine learning is an integral component of AI in customer service. This technology enables systems to improve their performance over time through experience. By continuously analyzing customer interactions, machine learning algorithms can identify trends and adjust their responses accordingly. This capability not only streamlines customer service processes but also enhances the quality of support provided. As machine learning evolves, its applications in customer service will likely expand, further revolutionizing the way businesses interact with their customers and respond to their needs.

Benefits of AI in Customer Interactions

Arti cial Intelligence (AI) has transformed customer interactions by enhancing the ef ciency and effectiveness of service delivery. One of the primary bene ts of AI in customer interactions is its ability to provide immediate assistance through chatbots and virtual assistants. These AI-driven tools are available 24/7, allowing customers to receive instant responses to their inquiries at any time. This immediacy not only improves customer satisfaction but also reduces the workload on human agents, enabling them to focus on more complex issues that require a personal touch.

Another signi cant advantage of AI in customer service is the ability to analyze vast amounts of data to personalize interactions. AI systems can aggregate and analyze customer data, including past purchases, preferences, and behaviors, to tailor responses and recommendations. This personalization fosters a deeper connection between the brand and its customers, enhancing loyalty and encouraging repeat business. By leveraging AI tools, companies can deliver targeted marketing messages and product suggestions that resonate with individual customers, ultimately driving sales and improving the overall customer experience.

AI also contributes to improved accuracy in customer service interactions. With natural language processing and machine learning capabilities, AI tools can understand and interpret customer queries more effectively than ever before. This leads to quicker resolutions, as AI can identify the intent behind customer requests and route them to the appropriate resources or provide accurate answers directly. By minimizing human error and delivering consistent responses, AI helps maintain a high standard of service that customers expect.

Furthermore, AI in customer interactions allows for continuous improvement through data collection and analysis. AI systems can track customer interactions and feedback, identifying patterns and trends that inform future strategies. This data-driven approach enables businesses to re ne their customer service processes, address common pain points, and enhance the customer journey. As companies adapt to these insights, they can stay ahead of customer expectations, fostering a culture of innovation and responsiveness.

Lastly, the integration of AI in customer interactions can lead to signi cant cost savings for businesses. By automating routine tasks and streamlining operations, companies can reduce the need for extensive customer service teams while maintaining, or even enhancing, service quality. This cost ef ciency allows businesses to allocate resources more strategically, investing in areas that further enhance customer satisfaction and long-term loyalty. As organizations continue to embrace AI technologies, the bene ts to customer interactions will undoubtedly grow, paving the way for a new era of customer service excellence.

Chapter 3: Implementing AI Solutions

Assessing Your Customer Service Needs

Assessing your customer service needs is a critical step in leveraging AI effectively. Understanding the speci c requirements of your business and its customers will allow you to implement AI solutions that are tailored to enhance the customer experience. Begin by evaluating your current customer service processes, identifying strengths and weaknesses. Analyze customer feedback, service response times, and overall satisfaction levels to gain insights into areas that require improvement. This foundational assessment will guide your decision-making as you explore AI applications that can address these gaps.

Next, consider the nature of your customer interactions. Different industries have varying demands when it comes to customer service. For instance, a retail business may require a robust chatbot for handling high volumes of inquiries, while a nancial institution might prioritize secure, personalized support channels. Identifying the speci c types of interactions your customers engage in will help you determine which AI tools are best suited to your needs. This analysis should also include an understanding of peak times and customer behaviors, enabling you to anticipate needs and allocate resources effectively.

Another important aspect of assessing your customer service needs is examining the skill sets of your current team. AI can augment human capabilities, but it is essential to recognize the areas where your staff might require additional training or support. Evaluate the current knowledge and technological pro ciency of your team to determine how AI can best t into your existing framework. This may involve upskilling employees to work alongside AI tools or rede ning roles to focus on more complex customer interactions that require human empathy and problem-solving.

Data analysis plays a vital role in assessing customer service needs. Collecting and analyzing customer data will provide insights into trends, preferences, and pain points. Utilize tools that track customer interactions across various channels to create a comprehensive picture of customer behavior. This data-driven approach will enable you to identify speci c areas where AI can streamline operations, reduce response times, or enhance personalization. By understanding how customers engage with your services, you can make informed decisions about AI implementations that will deliver tangible bene ts.

Lastly, it is crucial to continuously reassess your customer service needs as your business evolves and technology advances. The landscape of customer expectations is always changing, and staying ahead requires ongoing evaluation. Implement a feedback loop that allows you to gather input from customers and staff regularly. This will ensure that your AI solutions remain aligned with customer needs and preferences. By fostering a culture of adaptability and innovation, your business can effectively leverage AI to not only meet but exceed customer service expectations over time.

Choosing the Right AI Tools

Choosing the right AI tools for customer service is a critical decision that can greatly impact the ef ciency and effectiveness of support operations. With the rapid advancement of technology, numerous options are available, each offering unique features and capabilities. It is essential to assess the speci c needs of your organization and the expectations of your customers before making a choice. Understanding the different AI tools available in the market allows businesses to identify which solutions will align best with their service goals.

One of the rst considerations when selecting AI tools is the type of customer interactions they will support. For instance, chatbots are popular for handling basic inquiries and providing instant responses to common questions. However, more complex interactions may require advanced natural language processing (NLP) capabilities or AI-driven analytics that can interpret customer sentiment. Evaluating the nature of customer queries and the desired level of support will help businesses determine whether they need simple automation or more sophisticated AI solutions.

Integration capabilities are another crucial aspect to consider. The chosen AI tools should seamlessly integrate with existing customer relationship management (CRM) systems and other software applications utilized by the organization. This compatibility ensures that data ows smoothly between platforms, enabling a uni ed view of customer interactions. When AI tools can access historical customer data and previous interactions, they can provide more personalized and relevant responses, signi cantly enhancing the overall customer experience.

Scalability is also an important factor in choosing AI tools. As businesses grow and customer demands change, the selected tools must be able to adapt and scale accordingly. Organizations should look for solutions that can handle increased volumes of interactions without sacri cing performance. Additionally, the ability to incorporate new features or expand functionality over time is essential for future-proo ng AI investments.

Finally, assessing the level of support and resources provided by AI vendors is vital. The implementation of AI tools can be complex and may require training and ongoing support. Organizations should seek vendors that offer comprehensive onboarding assistance, technical support, and resources to ensure that staff can effectively utilize the tools. A strong partnership with the AI vendor can enhance the overall success of the implementation and lead to improved customer service outcomes. By carefully considering these factors, businesses can make informed decisions that leverage AI technology to elevate their customer service experience.

Integration with Existing Systems

Integration with existing systems is a critical component in the successful deployment of AI technologies in customer service. Organizations often operate with a variety of legacy systems, databases, and software platforms that handle different aspects of customer interactions. For AI solutions to be effective, they must seamlessly integrate with these existing systems to ensure a smooth ow of information. This integration facilitates a uni ed view of the customer, allowing AI tools to analyze data from multiple sources and provide insights that enhance service delivery.

One of the primary challenges in integrating AI with existing systems is the compatibility of technology. Legacy systems may use outdated protocols or formats that are not conducive to modern AI applications. Organizations must assess their current infrastructure and identify potential barriers to integration. This may involve upgrading certain components, implementing middleware solutions, or even migrating data to cloud-based platforms that support more exible integration. By investing in the right technology stack, businesses can create an environment where AI can thrive and add signi cant value to customer service processes.

Data silos pose another signi cant challenge in the integration process. When customer data is scattered across various departments or systems, it becomes dif cult for AI algorithms to access comprehensive datasets needed for accurate analysis. To combat this issue, organizations must adopt a strategy that promotes data centralization and standardization. This often involves creating a uni ed database or adopting customer relationship management (CRM) systems that consolidate data from different touchpoints. With centralized data, AI systems can gain deeper insights into customer behavior, preferences, and pain points, enabling more personalized service interactions.

Moreover, the integration process should prioritize interoperability and scalability. As businesses grow and evolve, their customer service needs will change, and the AI systems must adapt accordingly. By choosing integration solutions that are exible and scalable, organizations can ensure that their AI tools remain relevant and effective over time. This also includes selecting platforms that support API integrations, allowing for easy updates and the addition of new functionalities as they become necessary. A forward-thinking approach to integration will allow organizations to leverage the full potential of AI in enhancing customer service.

Finally, it is essential to involve all stakeholders in the integration process, from IT teams to customer service representatives. Engaging various departments ensures that the integration strategy aligns with the overall business objectives and addresses the speci c needs of different teams. Regular training and communication about the capabilities and bene ts of the integrated AI systems will foster a culture of collaboration and innovation. By taking a holistic approach to integration, organizations can harness the power of AI to deliver exceptional customer service that meets and exceeds customer expectations.

Chapter 4: Chatbots and Virtual Assistants

Understanding Chatbots

Chatbots have emerged as a transformative technology in the realm of customer service, rede ning how businesses interact with their clients. At their core, chatbots are automated conversational agents that utilize arti cial intelligence (AI) to engage with users. They can simulate human-like conversations, providing quick and ef cient responses to customer inquiries. This functionality enables businesses to offer round-the-clock support, ensuring that customers receive timely assistance regardless of the hour.

One of the primary advantages of chatbots is their ability to handle a multitude of queries simultaneously. Unlike human agents, who can only manage one conversation at a time, chatbots can engage with thousands of customers concurrently. This scalability not only improves response times but also alleviates the pressure on customer service teams. As a result, companies can maintain a high level of service quality during peak hours, ultimately leading to increased customer satisfaction and loyalty.

Chatbots can be categorized into two main types: rule-based and AI-driven. Rule-based chatbots operate on prede ned scripts and can only respond to speci c commands or questions. They are suitable for handling straightforward inquiries such as FAQs or basic troubleshooting. On the other hand, AI-driven chatbots leverage machine learning and natural language processing to understand context and intent, allowing them to provide more nuanced responses. This adaptability makes AI-driven chatbots better equipped to handle complex interactions, enhancing the overall customer experience.

The implementation of chatbots in customer service also generates valuable data that can inform business strategies. By analyzing customer interactions, companies can gain insights into common issues, preferences, and behaviors. This information can be used to improve products, re ne service offerings, and enhance marketing efforts. Additionally, chatbots can be programmed to collect feedback from users, providing businesses with direct insights into customer satisfaction and areas for improvement.

Despite their many advantages, the integration of chatbots into customer service is not without challenges. Some customers may prefer human interaction, particularly in complex or emotionally charged situations. To address this, businesses must nd a balance between automated support and human involvement. By clearly communicating the capabilities of chatbots and providing easy access to human agents when needed, companies can create a seamless customer experience that leverages the strengths of both AI and human support.

Designing Conversational Interfaces

Designing conversational interfaces is a critical aspect of leveraging AI in customer service. These interfaces serve as the rst point of interaction between customers and businesses, making it essential to create them with the user experience in mind. A well-designed conversational interface should be intuitive, responsive, and capable of understanding user intent. By focusing on these elements, companies can ensure that their AI-powered chatbots or virtual assistants provide meaningful and ef cient interactions that enhance customer satisfaction.

One key element in designing effective conversational interfaces is the choice of language and tone. The interface should communicate in a manner that aligns with the brand's voice while also being easily understandable to users. This requires a balance between professionalism and approachability. For instance, while a nancial institution might adopt a more formal tone, a lifestyle brand could engage users with a casual and friendly approach. Understanding the target audience is crucial in setting this tone, as it in uences how customers perceive the interaction and ultimately affects their overall experience.

Another important consideration is the ow of conversation. A well-structured dialogue not only guides users through their inquiries but also anticipates their needs. Designers should map out potential user journeys, identifying common queries and responses. By incorporating decision trees and fallback options, the interface can handle unexpected inputs gracefully. This ensures that users feel supported throughout their interaction, reducing frustration and increasing the likelihood of a successful resolution to their queries.

In addition to language and conversation ow, integrating feedback mechanisms into conversational interfaces can signi cantly enhance their effectiveness. Allowing users to provide feedback on their experience can offer valuable insights into areas for improvement. This could include options for users to rate their interactions or provide comments on the clarity and helpfulness of responses. Analyzing this feedback enables continuous re nement of the interface, ensuring it evolves in line with customer preferences and expectations.

Finally, accessibility plays a vital role in designing conversational interfaces. It is essential to consider users with varying abilities and preferences, ensuring that the interface is inclusive. This can involve implementing features such as voice recognition for those who may struggle with typing or providing text-to-speech capabilities for users with visual impairments. By prioritizing accessibility, businesses can create conversational interfaces that cater to a broader audience, thereby enhancing customer care and fostering loyalty in an increasingly competitive marketplace.

Real-World Applications of Chatbots

Chatbots have become integral to customer service across various industries, transforming how businesses interact with their customers. One of the most visible applications of chatbots is in the retail sector, where they assist customers in navigating product catalogs, checking stock availability, and processing orders. Retailers leverage chatbots to provide instant responses to customer inquiries, signi cantly reducing wait times and enhancing the shopping experience. This immediate access to information not only satis es customers but also frees up human agents to handle more complex queries.

In the banking and nancial services industry, chatbots play a crucial role in managing customer accounts and providing nancial advice. They can help users check their account balances, transfer funds, and even alert them to unusual spending patterns. By using chatbots, nancial institutions can offer 24/7 support, ensuring that customers can access essential services at any time. This continuous availability helps build trust and satisfaction among users, as they feel supported in managing their nances without the constraints of traditional banking hours.

The healthcare sector has also adopted chatbots to streamline patient interactions and improve service delivery. These intelligent systems can schedule appointments, provide medication reminders, and answer common health-related questions. By automating routine tasks, healthcare providers can allocate more time to patient care, thereby enhancing the overall quality of service. Moreover, chatbots can assist in triaging patients by gathering preliminary information about symptoms before a human professional intervenes, facilitating a more ef cient healthcare process. Travel and hospitality industries have embraced chatbots to enhance customer engagement and streamline booking processes. Travelers can interact with chatbots to book ights, make hotel reservations, and receive real-time updates about their itineraries. This immediate access to information helps reduce stress for travelers and improves overall satisfaction. Additionally, chatbots can provide personalized recommendations based on customer preferences, further enriching the travel experience and encouraging customer loyalty.

Education is another sector where chatbots are making a signi cant impact. Educational institutions utilize chatbots to assist students with enrollment processes, provide information about courses, and answer frequently asked questions. They can also facilitate tutoring sessions by guiding students through complex topics or providing resources for further learning. By incorporating chatbots into their services, educational institutions can enhance communication with students, making it easier for them to access the information they need, ultimately fostering a more supportive learning environment.

Chapter 5: Personalization Through AI

Data Collection and Analysis

In the realm of customer care, data collection and analysis serve as the backbone for understanding customer needs and enhancing service delivery. As organizations increasingly leverage arti cial intelligence, the methods of gathering and interpreting customer data have evolved. Traditional methods such as surveys and feedback forms are now complemented by advanced technologies that can analyze customer interactions in real-time. This transformation allows businesses to collect vast amounts of data from various channels, including social media, chatbots, and customer service calls, creating a comprehensive view of customer behavior and preferences.

Effective data collection begins with identifying the key metrics that inform customer service strategies. Companies can track customer satisfaction scores, response times, and resolution rates to gauge performance. Furthermore, AI-powered tools can analyze sentiment from customer interactions, providing insights into how customers feel about their experiences. This multidimensional approach to data collection ensures that businesses are not only gathering information but also understanding the nuances behind customer feedback. By focusing on relevant metrics, organizations can make informed decisions that enhance their service offerings.

Once data is collected, the next step involves rigorous analysis to extract actionable insights. Advanced analytics techniques, including machine learning algorithms, can identify patterns and trends that may not be immediately apparent through manual analysis. For example, predictive analytics can forecast future customer behaviors based on historical data, enabling businesses to proactively address issues before they escalate. Additionally, clustering techniques can segment customers into distinct groups, allowing for personalized service that meets the unique needs of each segment. This deep analysis empowers organizations to tailor their customer care strategies effectively.

Moreover, the integration of AI in data analysis enhances the speed and accuracy of insights derived from customer data. AI algorithms can process large datasets in a fraction of the time it would take a human analyst, revealing critical insights that drive strategic decision-making. This ef ciency not only improves the responsiveness of customer service teams but also enables continuous improvement based on real-time feedback. As AI systems learn from ongoing interactions, they become increasingly adept at recognizing emerging trends and adapting service protocols accordingly.

Ultimately, the combination of robust data collection and sophisticated analysis techniques positions organizations to deliver exceptional customer care. By leveraging AI, businesses can transform raw data into meaningful insights that inform their strategies and enhance customer experiences. This proactive approach to understanding customer needs fosters loyalty and satisfaction, positioning companies as leaders in the competitive landscape of customer service. Embracing these technologies is not just a trend; it is a crucial element in the evolution of customer care in the age of AI.

Creating Personalized Customer Experiences

Creating personalized customer experiences is essential in today's competitive landscape, and leveraging AI technologies plays a pivotal role in achieving this goal. Personalization can signi cantly enhance customer satisfaction, loyalty, and retention. AI tools can analyze vast amounts of data to understand individual customer preferences, behaviors, and needs, enabling businesses to tailor their offerings accordingly. By harnessing the power of AI, companies can move beyond generic interactions and create meaningful connections with their customers.

One of the most effective ways to create personalized experiences is through data analytics. AI can sift through customer data from various sources, such as purchase history, browsing behavior, and social media interactions, to uncover insights that would otherwise remain hidden. This analysis allows businesses to segment their customer base more accurately and develop targeted marketing campaigns that resonate with speci c groups. For instance, an AI-driven recommendation engine can suggest products that align with a customer's previous purchases, enhancing the shopping experience and driving sales.

In addition to data analytics, AI-powered chatbots and virtual assistants have transformed the way companies interact with customers. These tools can provide real-time assistance and personalized responses based on the customer's history and preferences. For example, when a customer reaches out for support, an AI system can quickly retrieve relevant information from previous interactions, enabling a more ef cient and tailored response. This level of personalization not only improves the ef ciency of customer service but also fosters a sense of understanding and care that customers increasingly expect.

Another critical aspect of creating personalized experiences is the importance of timely and relevant communication. AI can automate and optimize communication strategies, ensuring that customers receive the right message at the right time. By utilizing predictive analytics, businesses can anticipate customer needs and preferences, allowing them to send personalized offers or content that aligns with the customer's current interests. This proactive approach not only enhances the customer relationship but also increases the likelihood of conversion and repeat business.

Lastly, creating personalized customer experiences requires a culture of continuous improvement. Businesses must be willing to adapt their strategies based on customer feedback and evolving preferences. AI can facilitate this process by providing insights into customer sentiment and behavior, allowing companies to ne-tune their personalization efforts. By regularly analyzing data and adjusting their approaches, organizations can ensure that they remain relevant and continue to meet the ever-changing needs of their customers, ultimately leading to long-term success in the marketplace.

Case Studies of Successful Personalization

The implementation of personalization in customer service has been signi cantly enhanced through the use of arti cial intelligence, resulting in numerous success stories across various industries. One notable case is that of Amazon, which has leveraged AI algorithms to provide personalized product recommendations based on user behavior. By analyzing past purchases, browsing history, and customer reviews, Amazon creates a tailored shopping experience that not only encourages repeat visits but also increases average order values. This strategic use of AI ensures that customers feel understood and valued, fostering loyalty and driving sales.

Another exemplary case is Starbucks, which utilizes AI to personalize its customer engagement through the Starbucks Rewards program. By analyzing customer data, including purchase history and preferences, Starbucks can send personalized offers and recommendations through its app. This approach has led to a signi cant increase in customer engagement and retention, as users feel that the brand is catering speci cally to their tastes. The success of this personalization strategy is evident in the growth of the loyalty program, which has millions of active users and contributes a substantial portion of the company's revenue.

Sephora also stands out as a leader in customer service personalization through the use of AI. The beauty retailer employs a virtual artist feature in its mobile app, allowing customers to try on makeup virtually. By integrating AI with augmented reality, Sephora creates an engaging and personalized shopping experience, enabling customers to visualize products on themselves before purchase. This innovative approach not only enhances customer satisfaction but also reduces return rates, as customers are more likely to make informed decisions when they can see how products will look on them.

In the travel industry, Hilton Hotels has harnessed AI to re ne its customer service approach. The company utilizes AI-driven chatbots to provide personalized assistance to guests. These chatbots can analyze customer preferences and past interactions to offer tailored recommendations, such as room upgrades or dining options. This level of personalization not only improves the guest experience but also allows Hilton to streamline its operations, resulting in higher ef ciency and customer satisfaction ratings.

Finally, Net ix exempli es the power of AI in creating personalized content recommendations. By analyzing viewing habits and user ratings, Net ix employs sophisticated algorithms to suggest shows and movies tailored to individual tastes. This personalization not only enhances user engagement but also reduces churn rates, as subscribers are more likely to continue their memberships when they consistently nd content that resonates with their preferences. The success of Net ix's personalization strategy underscores the importance of leveraging AI to understand and meet customer needs effectively.

Chapter 6: Enhancing Customer Engagement

Predictive Analytics in Customer Interactions

Predictive analytics plays a crucial role in enhancing customer interactions by utilizing historical data to forecast future behaviors and preferences. In the realm of customer service, this technology enables organizations to anticipate customer needs, tailor interactions, and improve overall satisfaction. By analyzing patterns in customer data, companies can identify trends and make informed decisions that lead to more proactive and personalized service. This shift from reactive to predictive strategies allows businesses to address customer inquiries before they arise, ultimately fostering a more seamless experience.

One of the primary applications of predictive analytics in customer interactions is in understanding customer sentiment. By leveraging natural language processing and machine learning algorithms, companies can analyze customer feedback from various channels, such as social media, surveys, and support tickets. This analysis helps organizations gauge customer emotions and identify potential issues before they escalate. For instance, a sudden increase in negative sentiment about a product can prompt a company to investigate and address the underlying problems, thereby preventing customer churn and enhancing brand loyalty.

Moreover, predictive analytics facilitates targeted marketing efforts by segmenting customers based on their predicted behaviors. By identifying which customers are likely to respond positively to speci c promotions or product recommendations, businesses can create tailored marketing campaigns that resonate with individual preferences. This not only increases the ef ciency of marketing spend but also improves conversion rates, as customers receive relevant offers that align with their interests. Consequently, a more personalized approach to marketing fosters a stronger connection between the brand and its customers.

In addition to improving marketing and sentiment analysis, predictive analytics can optimize customer service operations. By forecasting call volumes and customer inquiries, organizations can allocate resources more effectively, ensuring that support teams are adequately staffed during peak times. This data-driven approach minimizes wait times and enhances the overall customer experience. Furthermore, predictive models can identify which customers are at risk of requiring support based on their purchase history or engagement patterns, enabling preemptive outreach and personalized follow-up.

Ultimately, the integration of predictive analytics into customer interactions not only enhances the ef ciency of service delivery but also builds deeper relationships between brands and consumers. By anticipating needs and personalizing experiences, businesses can create a customer-centric environment that fosters loyalty and drives long-term success. As organizations continue to adopt AI-driven solutions, the ability to leverage predictive analytics will become increasingly vital in shaping the future of customer service, ensuring that interactions are not only ef cient but also meaningful and engaging.

Automated Customer Feedback Systems

Automated customer feedback systems are rapidly transforming the landscape of customer service by harnessing the power of arti cial intelligence. These systems utilize algorithms and machine learning to gather, analyze, and interpret customer feedback in real-time, offering businesses invaluable insights into customer satisfaction and areas for improvement. By automating the feedback process, companies can ef ciently capture customer sentiments across various touchpoints, including surveys, social media, and online reviews, enabling them to respond to customer needs promptly and effectively.

One of the key advantages of automated customer feedback systems is their ability to process vast amounts of data quickly. Traditional methods of gathering feedback, such as manual surveys and focus groups, can be time-consuming and may not accurately represent the voice of the customer. In contrast, automated systems can aggregate feedback from multiple sources, providing a comprehensive view of customer opinions. Advanced analytics tools can then identify trends and patterns, allowing companies to make data-driven decisions that enhance service quality and customer experience.

Moreover, these systems often incorporate natural language processing (NLP) technologies, which enable them to understand and interpret human language in a nuanced way. This capability allows businesses to analyze open-ended feedback and extract meaningful insights that might be overlooked in quantitative data. For example, NLP can help identify recurring themes in customer comments, such as common complaints about a product or service, enabling companies to address issues more effectively. This level of understanding fosters a more empathetic approach to customer care, as businesses can tailor their responses based on the speci c concerns raised by their customers.

The integration of automated feedback systems also facilitates a continuous feedback loop, which is essential for maintaining high standards of customer service. By regularly collecting and analyzing customer feedback, businesses can adapt their strategies and offerings to meet evolving customer expectations. This proactive approach not only helps in resolving immediate issues but also builds long-term customer loyalty, as clients appreciate brands that listen and respond to their needs. Furthermore, the ability to track feedback trends over time allows organizations to measure the impact of changes made in response to customer input, ensuring that improvements are aligned with customer preferences.

In conclusion, automated customer feedback systems represent a signi cant advancement in customer service, leveraging AI to enhance the way businesses understand and respond to their customers. By streamlining the feedback process, providing deep insights through advanced analytics, and fostering a culture of continuous improvement, these systems empower organizations to deliver exceptional service. As companies increasingly adopt these technologies, the potential for enhanced customer satisfaction and loyalty will only grow, marking a new era in customer care that prioritizes responsiveness and personalization.

The Role of AI in Omnichannel Strategies

The integration of arti cial intelligence into omnichannel strategies is transforming the landscape of customer service. As businesses strive to provide a seamless experience across various platforms, AI plays a crucial role in ensuring that customer interactions are uid and cohesive. By utilizing AI-powered tools, organizations can collect and analyze data from multiple touchpoints, allowing them to understand customer preferences and behaviors better. This data-driven insight enables companies to tailor their services and communications, ultimately enhancing customer satisfaction and loyalty.

AI technologies, such as chatbots and virtual assistants, are essential components of effective omnichannel strategies. These tools can operate across different channels, including social media, websites, and mobile apps, offering consistent support and information to customers regardless of their chosen platform. The ability to provide immediate assistance not only improves response times but also reduces the workload on human agents. This ef ciency allows customer service teams to focus on more complex inquiries, further improving the overall service experience.

Personalization is another signi cant advantage of incorporating AI into omnichannel strategies. By analyzing customer data, AI can help businesses deliver tailored recommendations and content that resonate with individual preferences. For instance, AI can track a customer's previous interactions and suggest products or services based on their behavior. This level of personalization not only enhances the customer experience but also drives sales, as customers are more likely to engage with offerings that align with their interests.

Moreover, AI's predictive analytics capabilities enable businesses to anticipate customer needs and preferences. By analyzing historical data and trends, AI can forecast future behavior, allowing companies to proactively address potential issues or offer relevant solutions. This foresight enhances customer engagement and fosters a sense of trust, as customers feel understood and valued. As a result, businesses that leverage AI for predictive insights can gain a competitive edge in their respective markets.

Finally, the integration of AI into omnichannel strategies also facilitates effective performance measurement and optimization. AI tools can track and evaluate customer interactions across all channels, providing valuable metrics that help businesses assess their service quality. By identifying areas for improvement, organizations can re ne their strategies and ensure that they are meeting customer expectations consistently. This continuous improvement process, driven by AI insights, is vital for maintaining a high standard of service and adapting to the ever-evolving landscape of customer care.

Chapter 7: Challenges and Considerations

Common Pitfalls in AI Implementation

One of the most signi cant pitfalls in AI implementation within customer service is the lack of a clear strategy. Organizations often rush into adopting AI technology without fully understanding their customer service needs or how AI can address them. Without a well-de ned strategy, companies may implement solutions that do not align with their objectives, leading to wasted resources and unmet expectations. It is crucial for businesses to conduct a thorough assessment of their existing processes, identify speci c pain points, and de ne measurable goals before integrating AI into their customer service operations.

Another common issue is the underestimation of the importance of data quality. AI systems rely heavily on data to learn and make decisions. If the data used to train these systems is awed, biased, or incomplete, the resulting AI solutions may produce inaccurate or unhelpful outcomes. Companies must prioritize data cleansing and ensure they have access to comprehensive, high-quality datasets. This includes not only historical customer interaction data but also ongoing input from current customers to continuously re ne AI models and improve accuracy over time.

Moreover, organizations often overlook the need for employee training and buy-in when implementing AI technologies. Employees may feel threatened by AI, fearing that it will replace their roles rather than enhance their capabilities. This mindset can lead to resistance and poor adoption of AI tools. To mitigate this, businesses should invest in training programs that highlight how AI can assist employees in providing better customer service. By fostering a collaborative environment where AI is seen as a partner rather than a competitor, companies can enhance employee engagement and improve overall service delivery.

A failure to monitor and evaluate the performance of AI systems is another common pitfall. After the initial implementation, some organizations may neglect ongoing assessments of AI effectiveness. AI technology is not a set-it-and-forget-it solution; it requires continuous monitoring to ensure it meets evolving customer needs and company objectives. Regular performance evaluations, customer feedback, and adjustments based on real-world results are essential to maintaining the relevance and effectiveness of AI applications in customer service.

Lastly, many organizations underestimate the importance of ethical considerations and transparency in AI implementation. Consumers are increasingly concerned about how their data is used and how decisions are made by AI systems. Companies must be proactive in establishing clear policies regarding data privacy and algorithmic transparency. Failure to address these concerns can lead to customer distrust and reputational damage. By prioritizing ethical practices and maintaining open lines of communication with customers about AI usage, businesses can build trust and loyalty, ultimately enhancing the customer experience.

Ensuring Data Privacy and Security

In the realm of customer service, the integration of arti cial intelligence presents both opportunities and challenges, particularly concerning data privacy and security. Organizations that leverage AI technologies must prioritize the safeguarding of customer information to maintain trust and compliance with regulations. This commitment requires a comprehensive understanding of data privacy laws, such as GDPR and CCPA, which mandate stringent measures to protect personal information. By fostering a culture of transparency and accountability, companies can not only adhere to these regulations but also enhance their reputation among consumers.

To ensure data privacy, businesses must implement robust data governance frameworks. These frameworks should include policies and procedures that dictate how customer data is collected, stored, and processed. Organizations should conduct regular audits to assess compliance with these policies, identifying and addressing any vulnerabilities. Additionally, data minimization should be a guiding principle, ensuring that only necessary information is collected and retained. This reduces the risk of exposure and strengthens customer con dence in the organization's commitment to protecting their information.

Security measures must also be at the forefront of any AI-driven customer service strategy. Utilizing encryption technologies, rewalls, and secure access controls can protect sensitive data from unauthorized access and breaches. Moreover, organizations should invest in continuous monitoring and incident response strategies to detect and mitigate potential threats in real-time. Employee training on cybersecurity best practices is equally critical, as human error often represents a signi cant risk in data security. By cultivating a workforce that understands the importance of data protection, businesses can create a more secure environment for their customers.

Furthermore, organizations should consider the ethical implications of using AI in customer service. This involves implementing practices that respect customer privacy while leveraging data analytics to improve service delivery. Offering customers the option to opt-in or opt-out of data sharing can empower them and foster a sense of control over their personal information. Transparency about how AI systems utilize data is essential; customers should be informed about what data is collected, how it is used, and the bene ts they can expect in return. This approach not only aligns with ethical standards but also enhances customer loyalty and satisfaction.

Lastly, building a proactive approach to data privacy and security is crucial in an evolving digital landscape. As technology advances, so do the tactics employed by cybercriminals. Therefore, organizations must stay abreast of the latest security trends and adapt their strategies accordingly. Collaborations with cybersecurity experts and participation in industry forums can provide valuable insights into emerging threats and best practices. By committing to ongoing education and improvement in data privacy and security measures, companies can effectively protect their customers while harnessing the full potential of AI in customer service.

Balancing Automation and Human Touch

In the evolving landscape of customer service, the integration of automation through arti cial intelligence (AI) has transformed the way businesses interact with their customers. Automation offers ef ciency, speed, and accuracy, allowing companies to handle vast volumes of inquiries without the limitations faced by human agents. However, as organizations increasingly embrace AI, they must also recognize the importance of maintaining a human touch in their customer interactions. The balance between automation and human engagement is crucial for fostering strong customer relationships and ensuring satisfaction.

Automation can streamline many routine tasks, such as answering frequently asked questions, processing orders, and tracking shipments. By utilizing AI-driven chatbots and virtual assistants, companies can provide immediate responses, which signi cantly enhances the customer experience. Customers appreciate the convenience of having their questions answered quickly, especially outside of traditional business hours. This ef ciency not only improves service delivery but also allows human agents to focus on more complex issues that require nuanced understanding and empathy.

Despite the advantages of automation, there are inherent limitations to AI systems. For instance, while AI can ef ciently handle straightforward queries, it often struggles with complex situations that require emotional intelligence or personalized responses. Customers may seek reassurance or understanding that a machine simply cannot provide. In these instances, the human touch becomes essential. Human agents can empathize with customers, show genuine concern, and build rapport, which technology alone cannot replicate. This human connection is vital, especially in industries where trust and empathy are paramount.

Finding the right balance between automation and human interaction is not merely a technical challenge but also a strategic one. Businesses must assess which customer service tasks can be effectively automated and which require a human presence. Implementing a hybrid model that allows for seamless transitions between AI and human agents can enhance customer satisfaction. For example, a customer may begin their interaction with a chatbot for initial inquiries, but if the conversation becomes more intricate, the system can escalate the matter to a human representative. This approach ensures that customers receive the best of both worlds—speed and ef ciency combined with empathy and understanding.

Ultimately, the goal of any customer service strategy should be to create a positive experience that fosters loyalty and advocacy. Organizations that successfully balance automation with a human touch are better positioned to meet the diverse needs of their customers. By leveraging AI to handle routine tasks while empowering human agents to engage on a deeper level, companies can cultivate a customer-centric culture that not only drives satisfaction but also enhances their overall brand reputation. In this new era of customer care, blending technology with humanity will be the key to exceptional service.

Chapter 8: Measuring Success in AI-Driven

Customer Care

Key Performance Indicators (KPIs)

Key Performance Indicators (KPIs) are essential metrics that organizations utilize to gauge the effectiveness and ef ciency of their customer service operations, particularly when integrating arti cial intelligence. In the realm of AI in customer service, KPIs provide critical insights into how well AI technologies are meeting customer needs, enhancing service quality, and driving overall business outcomes. By establishing clear KPIs, businesses can not only track performance but also make informed decisions about where to allocate resources and how to re ne their customer service strategies.

One of the primary KPIs in AI-driven customer service is the response time. This metric measures how quickly customer inquiries are addressed, whether through chatbots or human agents. A reduced response time often correlates with higher customer satisfaction, as swift resolutions are a key expectation in today's fast-paced environment. Organizations leveraging AI can automate responses to frequently asked questions, allowing for immediate engagement and signi cantly improving overall response metrics.

Another important KPI is the resolution rate, which indicates the percentage of customer issues resolved during the rst interaction. This metric is particularly relevant when assessing the effectiveness of AI systems, as it re ects how well these technologies can understand and address customer concerns without the need for escalation. A high resolution rate suggests that AI implementations are successful in delivering accurate and relevant information, ultimately leading to enhanced customer loyalty and reduced operational costs.

Customer satisfaction scores (CSAT) are another vital KPI for evaluating the success of AI-enhanced customer service initiatives. These scores are typically gathered through direct feedback from customers after their interactions with service representatives or AI systems. Monitoring CSAT allows organizations to assess how well their AI tools are performing from the customer's perspective. Consistently high satisfaction scores indicate that customers feel their needs are being met, while low scores may signal areas where improvements are necessary, either in AI algorithms or human oversight.

Finally, tracking the cost per interaction is crucial for understanding the

nancial impact of AI in customer service. This KPI provides insights into how

much it costs to resolve customer inquiries, encompassing both direct costs associated with AI tools and indirect costs related to human labor. By analyzing this data, businesses can determine the return on investment for their AI initiatives and identify opportunities to optimize operations. In conclusion, KPIs play a pivotal role in guiding organizations toward achieving exceptional customer service through the strategic use of arti cial intelligence.

Analyzing Customer Satisfaction and Loyalty

Analyzing customer satisfaction and loyalty is essential for businesses aiming to enhance their customer service strategies, particularly in an era increasingly dominated by arti cial intelligence. Customer satisfaction refers to the degree to which a product or service meets the expectations of customers. In contrast, customer loyalty encompasses the likelihood of customers to continue engaging with a brand over time, often resulting from positive experiences. By understanding the relationship between these two concepts, organizations can better tailor their offerings and improve their interactions with consumers, ultimately leading to sustained success.

The integration of AI technologies in customer service has revolutionized the way businesses gather and analyze feedback. Traditional methods, such as surveys and focus groups, while still relevant, often fail to capture real-time sentiments and nuanced opinions. AI-driven tools, such as chatbots and sentiment analysis software, can process vast amounts of data from various sources, including social media, product reviews, and direct customer interactions. This allows companies to gain immediate insights into customer opinions, preferences, and pain points, which are crucial for enhancing satisfaction and fostering loyalty.

Customer satisfaction metrics, such as Net Promoter Score (NPS) and Customer Satisfaction Score (CSAT), provide valuable quantitative data that organizations can use to assess their service quality. AI can enhance the accuracy and ef ciency of these measurements by automating data collection and providing predictive analytics. For instance, machine learning algorithms can identify patterns in customer behavior, helping businesses recognize which factors contribute most signi cantly to satisfaction. This enables them to make informed decisions about where to allocate resources and how to improve their service offerings.

Loyalty programs have become a common strategy for businesses to cultivate repeat customers. However, understanding the effectiveness of these programs requires ongoing analysis of customer behavior and preferences. AI can facilitate this by analyzing customer engagement and identifying trends that may indicate shifting loyalty. For example, predictive analytics can forecast potential churn, allowing businesses to intervene with targeted offers or personalized communication. By leveraging AI, organizations can create more dynamic and responsive loyalty programs that resonate with customers on a deeper level.

In conclusion, the analysis of customer satisfaction and loyalty is critical in today's competitive landscape. With the advent of AI, businesses have unprecedented opportunities to gather and interpret data, leading to enhanced customer experiences. By employing advanced analytics and understanding the interplay between satisfaction and loyalty, organizations can not only meet but exceed customer expectations. This strategic approach ultimately fosters a loyal customer base, essential for long-term growth and success in the rapidly evolving marketplace.

Continuous Improvement and Adaptation

Continuous improvement and adaptation are foundational principles in customer service, particularly when leveraging arti cial intelligence (AI). As the landscape of customer expectations evolves, businesses must remain agile, consistently re ning their practices to meet and exceed these demands. Continuous improvement involves a systematic approach to identifying areas for enhancement, while adaptation emphasizes the need for exibility in strategies and tools. Together, these principles ensure that organizations not only keep pace with technological advancements but also stay in tune with customer sentiments.

AI technologies are rapidly changing the way businesses interact with their customers. Implementing AI solutions, such as chatbots and predictive analytics, provides opportunities for ef ciency and personalization. However, organizations must not consider the integration of AI as a one-time initiative. Instead, they should foster a culture of ongoing evaluation and re nement. Regular assessments of AI performance, customer feedback, and service outcomes can reveal valuable insights that drive further enhancements. This iterative process allows businesses to optimize their AI tools to better serve their customers' needs.

Furthermore, adaptation in customer service requires a keen awareness of changing customer behaviors and preferences. As customers become more tech-savvy, their expectations shift towards faster response times, personalized experiences, and seamless interactions across multiple channels. Businesses must be prepared to adapt their AI strategies in response to these trends. This might involve updating algorithms to incorporate new customer data, retraining models to improve accuracy, or expanding service capabilities to include emerging communication platforms. By embracing adaptability, companies position themselves to remain relevant and effective in delivering exceptional customer care.

The role of employee training in continuous improvement cannot be overlooked. While AI can automate various processes, human insight remains invaluable in interpreting data and making strategic decisions. Training programs that focus on enhancing employees' understanding of AI tools can signi cantly impact service quality. Employees who are well-versed in AI capabilities can leverage these technologies to provide more nuanced support, ultimately enhancing the customer experience. Investing in continuous education ensures that employees are not only pro cient in using AI but also capable of contributing to the organization's improvement initiatives.

In conclusion, continuous improvement and adaptation are essential for leveraging AI in customer service effectively. Businesses that commit to regularly evaluating their AI systems, understanding evolving customer needs, and investing in employee training will cultivate a responsive and innovative service environment. By prioritizing these principles, organizations can enhance their customer care strategies, resulting in increased satisfaction and loyalty. In a world where change is constant, the ability to adapt and improve will distinguish successful businesses in the competitive landscape of customer service.

Chapter 9: The Future of Customer Care

Trends Shaping the Landscape of Customer Service

The landscape of customer service is undergoing a signi cant transformation, driven by advancements in technology and evolving consumer expectations. One of the most notable trends shaping this landscape is the integration of arti cial intelligence (AI) into customer service operations. Businesses are increasingly adopting AI-driven tools such as chatbots and virtual assistants to enhance customer interactions. These technologies allow for 24/7 support and instant responses to customer inquiries, making it possible for companies to provide timely assistance while reducing operational costs.

Another key trend is the rise of omnichannel support, which provides customers with a seamless experience across various platforms. Customers today expect to engage with brands through multiple channels, including social media, email, live chat, and phone calls. By leveraging AI, companies can unify these channels, ensuring that customer data and interaction history are accessible across all platforms. This integration not only improves response times but also empowers customer service representatives with valuable insights, enabling them to offer personalized support.

Data analytics is also playing a crucial role in shaping customer service strategies. Organizations are harnessing the power of AI to analyze vast amounts of customer data to identify patterns and preferences. This data-driven approach allows businesses to anticipate customer needs, tailor their services, and improve overall satisfaction. Predictive analytics can even help companies proactively address potential issues before they escalate, leading to a more positive customer experience and fostering loyalty.

Furthermore, the focus on emotional intelligence in customer service is gaining traction. AI technologies are becoming more sophisticated in understanding and responding to human emotions. By employing sentiment analysis and natural language processing, businesses can better gauge customer sentiment during interactions. This understanding enables organizations to tailor their responses and build stronger connections with customers, ultimately enhancing their overall service experience.

Lastly, there is a growing emphasis on ethical considerations in AI deployment. As companies leverage AI to streamline customer service, they must also address concerns surrounding data privacy and security. Customers are increasingly aware of how their information is used, and businesses must demonstrate transparency and accountability in their practices. By prioritizing ethical AI use, companies can build trust with their customers, ensuring that technology enhances rather than undermines the customer service experience.

The Role of AI in Future Customer Interactions

The integration of arti cial intelligence into customer service is transforming the way businesses interact with their clients. AI technologies such as chatbots, virtual assistants, and machine learning algorithms are increasingly being adopted to enhance customer interactions. These tools not only streamline communication but also provide personalized experiences that are tailored to individual customer needs. As organizations seek to maintain a competitive edge, understanding the role of AI in future customer interactions becomes paramount.

One of the most signi cant advantages of AI in customer service is its ability to process vast amounts of data quickly and accurately. AI systems can analyze customer behavior, preferences, and feedback in real-time, allowing businesses to respond proactively to customer inquiries and issues. This data-driven approach enables companies to anticipate customer needs and offer solutions before problems escalate. Consequently, customers experience quicker resolutions and a more satisfying interaction, fostering loyalty and trust in the brand.

Moreover, AI is revolutionizing the personalization of customer experiences. Advanced algorithms can segment customers based on their history and preferences, enabling businesses to deliver tailored recommendations and communications. For instance, an AI-driven system might suggest products or services based on a customer's previous purchases or browsing behavior. This level of personalization not only enhances the customer experience but also increases the likelihood of repeat business, as clients feel understood and valued by the brand.

AI also plays a crucial role in enhancing ef ciency within customer service teams. By automating routine tasks, such as answering frequently asked questions or processing simple transactions, AI allows human agents to focus on more complex inquiries that require emotional intelligence and nuanced understanding. This shift not only improves the overall ef ciency of customer service operations but also empowers agents to provide higher-quality interactions, ultimately leading to improved customer satisfaction.

As businesses continue to adopt AI technologies, the future of customer interactions will likely be characterized by a seamless integration of human and AI capabilities. Companies that effectively leverage AI will not only enhance their operational ef ciency but also create a more engaging and personalized experience for their customers. Embracing this technological evolution will be essential for organizations aiming to thrive in an increasingly competitive landscape, making the understanding of AI's role in customer interactions a critical focus for the future.

Preparing for the Next Generation of Customer Care

As businesses evolve in the digital age, preparing for the next generation of customer care necessitates a thorough understanding of emerging technologies and evolving customer expectations. The integration of arti cial intelligence (AI) into customer service is no longer just an option; it has become a fundamental requirement for organizations seeking to maintain a competitive edge. Companies must invest in AI-driven tools and systems that enhance customer interactions, streamline processes, and provide personalized experiences. This preparation involves not only adopting new technologies but also retraining staff to work alongside these innovations and ensuring that their skills align with the capabilities of AI systems.

Understanding customer behavior is crucial in preparing for the future of customer care. Leveraging AI can provide organizations with valuable insights into customer preferences, pain points, and buying patterns. By analyzing large volumes of data, AI algorithms can identify trends and predict future behaviors, enabling companies to tailor their services accordingly. This customer-centric approach allows businesses to anticipate needs and proactively address issues, ultimately leading to increased satisfaction and loyalty. Organizations should focus on developing robust data analytics capabilities to harness this information effectively and ensure that the customer experience is both seamless and engaging.

Moreover, as AI technology advances, the need for ethical considerations in customer care becomes paramount. Companies must establish clear guidelines on how customer data is collected, stored, and used, ensuring transparency and trust. Customers are increasingly aware of privacy issues and are more likely to engage with brands that demonstrate a commitment to ethical practices. Training employees on these ethical standards and fostering a culture of responsibility within the organization will be essential in navigating the complex landscape of AI in customer service. By prioritizing ethical considerations, businesses can build stronger relationships with their customers and enhance their reputation in the market.

The implementation of AI in customer care also necessitates a shift in organizational structure. Traditional hierarchies may need to be reevaluated to promote collaboration between human agents and AI systems. This hybrid model allows for the strengths of both to be utilized effectively; while AI can handle routine inquiries and data processing, human agents can focus on complex issues that require empathy and nuanced understanding. Training programs should be designed to empower employees to excel in this new environment, equipping them with the skills to leverage AI tools while maintaining a human touch in customer interactions.

Finally, ongoing assessment and adaptation will be critical as customers' needs and technologies continue to evolve. Businesses should implement feedback mechanisms to gather insights from both customers and employees regarding their experiences with AI-driven customer care. Regularly reviewing these insights will allow organizations to make necessary adjustments, ensuring that their customer care strategies remain relevant and effective. Embracing a mindset of continuous improvement will not only enhance customer satisfaction but also position companies as leaders in the rapidly changing landscape of customer service. By preparing for the next generation of customer care, organizations can create exceptional experiences that foster lasting customer relationships.

Chapter 10: Conclusion and Next Steps

Recap of Key Insights

In the rapidly evolving landscape of customer service, the integration of arti cial intelligence has emerged as a transformative force. One of the key insights from this exploration is the necessity for organizations to embrace AI not merely as a tool but as a strategic partner in enhancing customer interactions. AI systems, such as chatbots and virtual assistants, can handle a substantial volume of inquiries simultaneously, enabling businesses to provide timely responses. This shift not only streamlines operations but also frees human agents to focus on more complex and nuanced customer needs, ultimately leading to a more ef cient service model.

Another critical insight is the importance of personalization in customer service. AI's ability to analyze vast amounts of customer data allows businesses to tailor their interactions based on individual preferences and behaviors. By leveraging machine learning algorithms, companies can predict customer needs and offer personalized solutions, thereby improving customer satisfaction and loyalty. This level of customization fosters a deeper connection between the brand and its customers, making them feel valued and understood, which is essential in today's competitive marketplace.

Moreover, the role of AI in data analytics cannot be overstated. Organizations can utilize AI to gather and interpret customer feedback in real-time, enabling them to identify trends and areas for improvement quickly. This proactive approach allows businesses to adapt their strategies based on customer insights, ensuring that they remain relevant and responsive to changing demands. By continually re ning their service offerings through data-driven decision-making, companies can enhance their overall customer experience and build a strong reputation in the market.

Additionally, the ethical implications of AI in customer service are becoming increasingly prominent. As organizations leverage AI technologies, they must remain vigilant about data privacy and security. Transparency in how customer data is used and ensuring robust protection measures are essential to building trust with customers. Companies that prioritize ethical practices not only comply with regulations but also differentiate themselves in a crowded market, reinforcing their commitment to customer care.

Lastly, the signi cance of human-AI collaboration stands out as a crucial insight. While AI can handle routine queries and tasks, the human touch remains irreplaceable in delivering exceptional customer service. Training staff to work alongside AI systems enhances their ability to resolve complex issues, fostering a hybrid model where technology and human empathy coexist. This synergy between AI and human agents can create a more holistic service experience, ultimately driving customer satisfaction and loyalty in a world increasingly reliant on technology.

Developing an Action Plan for Implementation

Developing an action plan for implementing AI in customer service is essential for organizations aiming to enhance their customer interactions and streamline operations. The rst step in crafting this action plan is to de ne clear objectives. These objectives should align with the overall business goals and address speci c customer service challenges. By identifying what the organization hopes to achieve—whether it's reducing response times, increasing customer satisfaction, or automating routine inquiries—teams can create a focused approach that guides the adoption of AI technology.

Once objectives are established, the next phase involves assessing current customer service processes and technology. Organizations should conduct a thorough analysis of existing work ows, tools, and customer interaction points. This evaluation helps identify areas where AI can add value, such as through chatbots, predictive analytics, or personalized service recommendations. Understanding the current landscape allows teams to pinpoint gaps and opportunities, ensuring that the AI solutions implemented will effectively address real-world challenges faced by customer service representatives.

After understanding the current processes, organizations should prioritize the AI initiatives based on feasibility, impact, and resource availability. Prioritization ensures that the most pressing issues are tackled rst and that efforts are not spread too thin. It is important to consider both short-term wins and long-term strategic goals. For instance, implementing a chatbot for frequently asked questions might yield quick results in ef ciency, while developing a more complex AI-driven analytics platform could provide deeper insights over time. Establishing a timeline for each initiative also helps in managing expectations and keeping teams aligned.

Equally important is the aspect of training and change management. Introducing AI tools requires not only technical implementation but also a cultural shift within the organization. Employees need to be equipped with the knowledge and skills to utilize AI effectively in their roles. This may involve training sessions, workshops, or ongoing support as they adapt to new systems. Additionally, fostering a culture that embraces innovation and AI technology will ease resistance and enhance collaboration between human agents and AI systems, ultimately leading to better service outcomes.

Finally, organizations must establish metrics for success and a feedback mechanism to evaluate the effectiveness of the AI initiatives. By setting speci c KPIs related to customer satisfaction, response times, and operational ef ciency, teams can measure the impact of the implemented solutions. Regular feedback loops with both employees and customers will provide insights into areas for improvement and enable organizations to re ne their approach continuously. This iterative process not only enhances the effectiveness of AI in customer service but also ensures that the technology evolves in alignment with changing customer needs and expectations.

Resources for Further Learning

In the rapidly evolving landscape of customer service, staying informed about the latest trends and technologies is crucial for professionals seeking to enhance their skills and knowledge. Numerous resources are available for those interested in the intersection of arti cial intelligence and customer service. Books, articles, and research papers provide foundational knowledge as well as cutting-edge insights. For instance, texts such as "Arti cial Intelligence for Customer Experience" offer a comprehensive overview of AI applications in service environments, while scholarly articles often delve into speci c case studies and industry analyses.

Online courses and webinars are another effective way to deepen your understanding of AI in customer service. Platforms like Coursera, Udemy, and LinkedIn Learning host a variety of courses focusing on AI technologies, machine learning, and their application in customer support scenarios. These courses often include hands-on projects, allowing learners to apply theories in practical situations. Additionally, many industry experts and organizations host webinars that cover current trends, challenges, and best practices, providing real-time insights and opportunities for interaction with thought leaders.

Networking and community engagement play a vital role in furthering one's understanding of AI applications in customer service. Joining professional organizations such as the Customer Service Institute or the International Customer Management Institute can connect individuals with peers and mentors. These organizations often host conferences, workshops, and local meetups that facilitate knowledge sharing and collaboration on innovative practices. Online forums and social media groups dedicated to customer service and AI can also serve as valuable platforms for discussion and resource exchange.

For those who prefer auditory learning, podcasts have become a popular medium for exploring AI in customer service. Numerous podcasts feature interviews with industry experts, discussions on the latest technologies, and insights into best practices. Listening to these discussions can provide both inspiration and practical advice. Podcasts such as "AI in Business" and "The Customer Service Secrets" are particularly noteworthy, as they cover relevant topics in an accessible format, allowing listeners to stay informed while multitasking.

Lastly, staying updated with industry publications and news outlets can greatly enhance your understanding of AI in customer service. Subscribing to newsletters from reputable sources like Harvard Business Review, McKinsey & Company, or industry-speci c journals can provide ongoing education and awareness of the latest trends and case studies. These publications often feature in-depth analyses and expert opinions that can guide strategic decisions and inspire innovative approaches in customer care. Engaging with these resources will equip professionals with the tools necessary to excel in an increasingly AI-driven customer service environment.

Customer Care 2.0: Leveraging AI for Exceptional Service

The rise of social media in the 21st century further

transformed customer service, creating a public forum for

interactions between consumers and brands. Customers

began to expect immediate responses to their inquiries

and complaints, leading companies to adopt more

proactive strategies. Social media platforms became both

a channel for customer service and a space for brand

reputation management. Businesses that effectively

engaged with customers on these platforms were able to

build stronger relationships and foster loyalty. As a result,

customer service evolved from a purely transactional

interaction to a more holistic experience that incorporated

brand values and customer engagement.

Delroy Briscoe

www.ingramcontent.com/pod-product-compliance
Lightning Source LLC
Chambersburg PA
CBHW071031050326
40689CB00014B/3602